A Living Sacrifice
for Jesus

A Living Sacrifice for Jesus

Regina Reyna

authorHOUSE®

AuthorHouse™
1663 Liberty Drive
Bloomington, IN 47403
www.authorhouse.com
Phone: 1-800-839-8640

First published by AuthorHouse   02/20/2012

ISBN: 978-1-4634-4523-2 (sc)
ISBN: 978-1-4634-4522-5 (ebk)

Library of Congress Control Number: 2012903371

Printed in the United States of America

Any people depicted in stock imagery provided by Thinkstock are models, and such images are being used for illustrative purposes only.
Certain stock imagery © Thinkstock.

This book is printed on acid-free paper.

To my wonderful husband, Rene Reyna, who has been there with me through it all.
I am so proud of you. I love you and am grateful the Lord brought us together.

This sickness will not end in death but it will be to glorify my son.
—John 11:4NIV

Let me begin by saying that I pray you know Jesus as your personal Savior. If not, it is not too late for you. All you have to do is say a prayer and ask Jesus into your heart. Know that He is the son of God and ask Him to wash away all your sins. Amen! This righteousness from God comes through faith in Jesus Christ to all who believe. There is no difference for all have sinned and fall short of the glory of God, and are justified freely by his grace through the redemption that came by Christ Jesus. God presented him as a sacrifice of atonement, through faith in his blood. He did this to demonstrate his justice, because in his forbearance he had left the sins committed beforehand unpunished he did it to demonstrate his justice at the present time, so as to be just and the one who justifies those who have faith in Jesus (Rom. 3:22-26) NIV I pray that you prayed that prayer—and welcome to our Father's kingdom! The angels are rejoicing over you, welcoming you into His kingdom! The angels are rejoicing over you, welcoming you in His presence! I would like to share with you the wonderful testimony that Jesus has blessed me with.

My journey with the Lord began when I got to Germany. I was diagnosed with breast cancer, and I had to go through the trial of chemotherapy and radiation. Jesus told me this sickness was not to harm me but to purify. Whatever comes into your body, Jesus will remove it.

> *They shall take up serpents; and if they drink any deadly thing, it shall not hurt them;*
> *they shall lay hands on the sick and they shall recover.* (Mark 16:18) KJV

The Lord gave me strength through the chemotherapy and radiation. The Lord said that death would not come to me, that I would instead awe and astonish the doctors and thus have a story to tell.

Some days were hard, and when my body ached all over, I would cry out to Jesus. Instantly He would take the pain away. I look back, and it seems such a long time ago. Jesus is so awesome and mighty. Jesus got me through by His word, and I live in His word. He showed me every healing scripture. I would read the scriptures until the words were flowing out of me. The doctors thought I was in denial. I would dance and sing in the hospital room. They would tell me that this was serious. A nurse would tell me to read books about breast cancer. I did not need books about breast cancer, as they were not going to heal me. Jesus has the healing power. Jesus healed and restored me to health. I know my father as Jehovah Rapha. His words nourished my body and brought health to my bones.

This will bring health to your body and nourishment to your bones. (Prov. 3:8) NIV

Jesus not only healed me; He made me whole. I am no longer the same person. Regina passed away; I am a new Regina in Christ.

> *I have been crucified with Christ, and I no longer live, but Christ lives in me. The life I live in the body, I live by faith in the Son of God, who loved me and gave himself for me.* (Gal. 2:20) NIV

Jesus is a healer today, yesterday, and forever, all glory. Yes, I battled the trial of breast cancer. I went through the chemotherapy and radiation, but each time I came out stronger in the word. The cancer did not defeat me but made me into the person I am now. Jesus is wonderful and awesome! Jesus took this broken person and saw something in her that she did not see. Jesus knew the plan He had for me way before I was born or even thought of.

> *Even though I walked through the valley of the shadow of death, I will fear no evil, for you are with me; your rod and your staff, they comfort me. You prepare a table before me in the presence of my enemies. You anoint my head with oil; my cup overflows. Surely goodness and love will follow me all the days of my life, and I will dwell in the house of the Lord forever.* (Ps. 23:4-6) NIV

As a living sacrifice, I offer my testimony as to what Jesus has done for me. He is no respecter person. He can do the same for you. In any situation or circumstances, nothing is too hard for our Father.

> *Heaven is His throne and earth is His footstool.* (Isa. 66:1) NIV

I pray that His healing is anointing and flowing wherever you may be. I pray that Jesus will touch you right now where you are and heal you from the top of your head to the soles of your feet. Let the anointing power pour over you and run over. It says this in His word:

> *Surely he hath borne our griefs, and carried our sorrows; yet we did esteem him stricken, smitten of God, and afflicted. But he was wounded for our transgressions; he was bruised for our iniquities: the chastisement of our peace was upon him.* (Isa. 53:4-5) KJV

Honor in Jesus' name. Amen!

Chapter 1

O my God, I trust in thee: let me not be ashamed,
let not mine enemies triumph over me.
—Ps. 25:2KJV

I was praying unto the Lord, asking Him for guidance in writing this book. For it is not about me; it is all about Jesus. We can do nothing without the Lord. He is the bread I need. I thirst for His hands to guide me through every day. When I was going through my trial, the enemy would come in like a flood, trying to discourage me. The enemy whispered in my ears that nothing the Lord told me was true, and that I was not healed. The enemy said that with every little ache and pain, it would come back. However, I remembered that Jesus has given us power and dominion over the enemy in His name. It is time for us to raise a standard against the enemy and stand up for Jesus' word. I don't know about you, but I know that it is time to speak God's word. Worship Him in spirit and in truth! Know that when He says it is done, it is done, and no weapon formed against you shall prosper. (Isa. 54:17)

I am going to be real with you. I have tried to read books about breast cancer, and all they contained was medical terminology. I want you to hear my testimony, and that is how to get through something like this—with Jesus! Let me tell you that through this trial, you cannot sit back at church and ask why you are there. You are there to praise the Lord because praise is your weapon. So get ready, bring out your praise, and shut the devil up! Praise and worship His mighty name, for He is worthy of your praise. Praise will change the atmosphere and give you strength. He desires to do so much in your life that He is reaching out to you with His arms open wide, saying, "Trust in me, for I am able to set you free!"

For I know the thoughts that I think toward you, saith the Lord, thoughts of peace, and not of evil, to give you an expected end. (Jer. 29:11) KJV

Do you hear that? An expected end! *Trust in the Lord with all thine heart and lean not unto thine own understanding* (Prov. 3:5) KJV It is wonderful when you hear your Father say that it is finished, that it won't come back, that he is your physician! Stand on Jesus' word. It is time to step out in faith and trust in His word. *Walk by faith, not by sight.* (2 Cor. 5:7) KJV

Let go and let God! Do not let the enemy steal your joy and place fear in your life. God does not want us to have fear, just a joy that overpasses every fear and doubt. Jesus wants to embrace you with His love and open doors that you would not even imagine. I remember when God told me that I was going to see so much more, that this was nothing. He will never leave me nor forsake me. I cannot even imagine what He is going to show me, because healing me was so awesome and mighty. I saw His hands on my life. There is so much more He wants to show you.

Yes, you are so special in His eyes, children of Christ! Have faith in God and nothing is impossible for Jesus. Look up at the sky and count all the stars. Abraham did, and God told him that that is how many descendents he would have. Abraham stood on faith. Whatever God says He will do, He will do, for He is an awesome and mighty God. You may be asking why me. As Jesus told me and I tell you, this is happening because the Lord wants you to lean on Him and to trust in Him with all your heart. Then when He is finished molding you, everything else will fall into place.

> *Beloved think it not strange concerning the fiery trial which is to try you, as though some strange thing happened unto you: but rejoice, inasmuch as ye are partakers of Christ's sufferings; that, when his glory shall be revealed, ye may be glad also with exceeding joy.*
> (1 Pet. 5:12-13) KJV

Do not lose sight of your victory! Sometimes things happen in life that we may not understand, and we need to trust in Jesus. Also know that Jesus knows what He is doing. No matter what is going on in your life, Jesus will give you the answer that you need.

> *Ask and it will be given to you; seek and you will find: knock and the door will be opened to you.* (Matt. 7:7) NIV

The Lord told me, "I chose you." He knew this day would come; He knew of this plan long before the world began. It was through this trial that I was set free. It delivered me from the enemy. Do not be discouraged, for Jesus has you in His hands. Commit to His word. Commit to God. To die with Christ is to be born again. To suffer is to make us right for a purpose. Whatever Jesus says, hold on to His promises; He is faithful. Jesus' promises are real, and He loves you. Amen.

I remember going to church when I was going through the chemotherapy. I was losing my hair, I was crying, and the Lord kissed me on the forehead. I instantly realized it hurt Him more than it hurt me. Do not ever think that Jesus does not hurt for you; it hurts Him more than anyone else. That is why He took our sins on Calvary. He knew that sin would bring hurt and pain, and because of Jesus, we are set free. I can imagine Jesus with tears running down His cheeks. I feel His warm and loving presence. I cannot help but praise and magnify His precious name. Jesus gave me so many encouraging words. The Lord told me to write down everything. He told me that it was not just for me but also for you. Do not fear, for Jesus is with you, and He is going to bless you in so many ways. Jesus is so good, awesome, and mighty. Never again will I have to fear. It is done. It is finished. I have been restored, and I have the victory! When you have the victory, it is done. It is finished in Jesus' name! I believe that every person who reads this book will be healed and set free in Jesus' mighty name!

> *I ask you, therefore, not to be discouraged because of my sufferings for you, which are your glory.* (Eph. 3:13) NIV

Know that He is all dominion. Trust, I say, in the Lord!

Notes

Notes

_____
_____
_____
_____
_____
_____
_____
_____
_____
_____
_____
_____
_____
_____
_____
_____
_____
_____
_____
_____
_____
_____
_____
_____
_____
_____
_____
_____
_____
_____
_____
_____
_____
_____
_____
_____

Chapter 2

Thou art snared with the words of thy mouth,
thou art taken with the words of thy mouth.
—Prov. 6:2KJV

Let me begin at the beginning. My sister-in-law was diagnosed with breast cancer at age twenty-eight, and from then on, I started wondering about me. Talking to my husband one day, I said, "What if I get breast cancer and have to have both breasts removed?" See, I opened the door for the enemy to come in. Watch what you say with your mouth. It is a powerful weapon, but glory be to Jesus. What the enemy meant for evil, Jesus turned into His glory!

One day I was watching a movie in which a woman was giving herself a breast exam. I was lying on the couch and decided to check myself. I felt two lumps: one on the left side of my breast and one in my left armpit. Deciding to get myself checked, I made a doctor appointment. At this point, we were stationed in Fort Hood, Texas. When I saw the doctor, she noted my age and said it was just fibroids. I went home, but my spirit was still not right.

Something would not let me accept that answer. However, I left it alone and decided to have it checked again at my next Pap smear exam. That would have been a year from that date. I know now that that was not the place Jesus wanted me to have the surgery. He wanted me to have the best. It was all in His timing. We were getting ready to move to Germany, and I was in Houston, seeing my family before we left. I noticed the lump on my breast had a red rash, so I decided to get it checked again as soon as I got to Germany. The Lord lets you know something is not right. I was having nightmares, and evil spirits were tormenting me in my dreams. I did not have rest in my spirit, and I knew that something was not right. I had an overwhelming fear and could not sleep in peace. My husband thought I was going crazy. I was not living for Jesus at that time, even though I knew what it was to be a Christian. You think that as long as you go to church on Sunday and are a good person, then you will make it to heaven. The devil is a liar. It is not just being a Christian on Sunday—but every day of your life.

Let me get back to what I was saying. So I went to the doctor, and he said we should get it checked to be on the safe side. He sent me to Krankenhause, a German hospital, to get an ultrasound. When they did the ultrasound, they said it did not look good and wanted to do a mammogram. At that point, I was on the edge of a cliff. I felt as if I were falling and did not know how to get myself out of the situation. I prayed to Jesus to take the feeling away. I remember going to the chapel and walking in, but still I did not feel complete. People told me it would be okay. I just knew something was not right. I cried for Jesus every day, fasted, and did everything to wake me up from the nightmare. I was so worried and going out of my mind. I just wanted the nightmare to be over. I went in the next week to get a mammogram. They said it looked suspicious. They did an ultrasound again, but something was different with this one. I turned to look at it and saw an evil skull face where the bump was, so I knew something was wrong. The enemy was trying to take me out.

Even when I was a little girl and knew that Jesus had something for me to do here on this earth, it was not time for me to go but was just the beginning. All I could do was cry and pray that this nightmare would be over. It was so overwhelming. Even writing this book is overwhelming. It brings back those feelings, but in Jesus' name, I bind up the fear right now. This book is not about me; it's all about Jesus. Jesus sustained me. He got me through.

They made an appointment for a biopsy, and the doctor told my husband and me what they were going to do. All I could do was cry and wish it were all a dream; it was my worst nightmare. When we left, we were numb inside. I looked at my husband and my little boy and wondered if I would see him grow up. Would I grow old with my husband? I was so terrified, and the enemy was attacking left and right. All I could do was cry out for Jesus. I knew that He would heal me. He was the only one who could set me free and deliver me from my enemies.

In the parking lot where we'd stopped at the grocery store, my husband broke down crying, and we cried and held each other's hands. In the car, we must have been thinking the same thing, but Jesus showed up at that right time. My husband saw a car pass by that said ONLY GOD on the back of the car window. After that, my husband wasn't worried. I didn't understand. I thought that everything was going to be over, but I now know Jesus was saying that only God could handle it and to leave it to Him. The next week, we went to get a biopsy and an MRI. They said it did look like cancer, and they would find out from the biopsy results. We went home to wait until the following week. While at home, we got all our furniture. I thought at the time that it was Jesus giving me something to keep me busy. My Bible was packed up, but it finally arrived. It was as if Jesus had placed the words right in my hands. When I look back, I know that it was all Him.

When the weekend was over, we went to get the results. They sent us upstairs to see the doctor. I was so scared. Have you ever put on a heavy backpack and it just weighed you down? That is exactly how I felt. My stomach was in knots. I was praying, and the fear was overwhelming. They finally called our name, and the doctor said that it was cancer. They wanted to remove it and, if possible, the lymph nodes. They did not know for sure if they had to remove lymph nodes, so we had to decide whether to do it in Germany or go home to the States. I was in a foreign country, miles away from my family, and had no idea what to do. I told my husband that Jesus sent us to Germany for a reason, so let us do it in Germany. We went back into the doctor's room, but it seemed like a nightmare that would never end.

Yet I had complete peace in Germany. I knew that Jesus was with us in that hospital room. We were not alone; Jesus was holding us in His arms, letting me know that everything was all right. "I have you in my arms. Have no fear. I am with you. Very soon, you will understand everything I have for you and your family!" We told the doctor that we would have the surgery in Germany. I had no idea what was going to happen, and I did not do any research. I have no idea what any of the medical terminology is. Jesus did not want me to look at that. I tried to discover what kind of cancer it was by reading books, but Jesus would ask me what I was doing. He wanted me to walk in faith and not by sight. If you were to ask me any medical terminology, all I could tell you is that Jesus healed me, took care of me, and gave me the best. That is what walking in faith and not by sight is—trusting in Jesus with all our hearts and not trying to figure it out ourselves.

They set a date for the surgery, just two days after the results. I started to pray and ask Jesus to heal me. I started reading my Bible and felt so much better and excited because I knew that Jesus had a plan for me. I remember praying that when they went into surgery, they would find nothing. Jesus knew that I would not change; it had to take this trial to purify me.

When I went into surgery, I was not scared at all. I was not nervous. I had a peace that overcame every fear. I know that Jesus was with me, and that is why peace was with me. The doctors and the nurses asked me if I was nervous, and I said no. They could not believe it. They thought I would be scared being in a foreign country, but I knew Jesus was with me. I know now that it was His desire to have the surgery in Germany. Whatever He brings together will not fail, for He was in that surgery room. It was not the doctors who healed me; it was Jesus. Everything that was not of Jesus in you I took out, and I make no mistakes! For I created heaven and the earth, and I created you in your mother's womb and knew you even before you were born and already knew your destiny.

Notes

_____

_____

_____

_____

_____

_____

_____

_____

_____

_____

_____

_____

_____

_____

_____

_____

_____

_____

_____

_____

_____

_____

_____

_____

_____

_____

_____

_____

_____

_____

_____

_____

_____

_____

_____

_____

_____

_____

_____

Notes

Chapter 3

He has put a new song in my mouth, a hymn of Praise to our God.
Many will see and fear and put their trust in the Lord.
—Ps. 40:3NIV

Back in my room, I felt ready to get up and walk. We waited for the doctors to come in and tell us how the surgery went. We also wanted to find out if the cancer was in my lymph nodes. Because my arm was numb, I suspected that they had taken out lymph nodes. I was hoping that Jesus had healed me and I did not need to have chemotherapy or radiation. Before the surgery, I received scriptures about healing and restoration, so I believed that it was over, and that all I needed was the surgery. But Jesus had different plans, and His ways are higher than our ways.

I had no pain after the surgery. I felt I could go home that same day and get back to my life. I felt a release, and I wanted to get back to life. However, Jesus did not want me to get back to my old life. He wanted me to change and be a new creation in Christ—not the same Regina but a new Regina in Christ Jesus. He knew I would have to go through the trial to open my eyes to change and do His will. He had my steps ordered. Jesus gives you the strength to endure and know that your steps are ordered. He is going to blow your mind. Follow His ways and watch how He transforms your life. You will never desire the old you, but you will desire to be all that Jesus wants you to be. Most of all, you will just want to be in His presence.

The doctors came in, and there were about six or seven looking at me as if I were finished. I felt peace through it all and knew that Jesus was in that room, rubbing my cheeks and saying, "Daughter, everything is all right. Trust in me, not in men." The doctors said they had to remove the lymph nodes, and it sounded as if they said one lymph node had cancerous cells. They would have to examine them in a laboratory, and I would get my results on Monday. Then they left. I just stayed quiet, knowing that Jesus would get me through. I knew I was healed, and I gave Him all the glory.

My husband came in a little after the doctors left. I would not tell him what the doctors had said, but I was so happy to see my family. They brought joy to my face. My husband did not speak a lot. Men are different in dealing with emotions. I always looked to people for advice, and I always put everyone above Jesus. Now I was putting Jesus above everyone else, including my husband. I talked to Jesus about everything: my fears, doubts, and questions. I hardly talked to my husband about these things. The only person that had the answers was Jesus. My husband was distant, and I know it was hard on him. All along, Jesus was speaking to him as well. Jesus was comforting my husband and me, embracing us in His love. Even though we were not worthy of His love, He loved us so much. He saved us. Your trial is not to defeat you or your family but to make you stronger!

The next day, I was very down and thinking, Why me? I was so worried, and all kinds of thoughts were going through my head. I felt so empty inside, so lost. As a child, did you ever get lost in a mall or a store and couldn't find your parents or a loved one? You have that fear as you are looking for them, crying and wondering if you will ever see them again. I had that fear. Would I see my son grow up? Would I have more children? Would I grow old with my husband? Would I be able to live a life that was worthy in Jesus' eyes? I looked back at how meaningless my life was, and I wanted to do things differently, to not live for this world but to live showing Jesus love. I wanted to reach out to others and have my Father say, "Well done. I am so proud of you."

I woke up crying. The nurses came in and began telling me some things I do not remember. But it did not make me feel better. Then they told me I had to take more tests. They had to check my bones, liver, and heart. Therefore, our flesh starts thinking the worst. I was already afraid of test results and did not want any more done. I was so terrified and scared and just had sadness all around me. I felt empty inside. When my husband came, he saw how sad I was, and he took a picture of me in the hospital and showed it to me. I started to cry. All I saw was darkness—no light. It actually looked like a dull black-and-white picture show. No life! No light! The enemy thought he was getting to me. The enemy was all around me, whispering in my ear. All those lies. He is nothing but a liar. All he was trying to do was steal, kill, and destroy.

My husband told me about Joseph, how God got him out of all his trials and took him to the destiny God had for him. Jesus will get His word out to you through anyone and anybody. My husband and I did not truly know the Lord at the time, yet He spoke to us and gave us His word. I told my husband that he was right.

My husband was leaving to go get something to eat with our son. I kissed both of them, and when they left, I decided that I needed to tell my husband to buy me a CD player. Jesus knew music ministered to me. I love hearing praise music. So Jesus sent my husband and son back to the room. I heard my son's little feet running through the halls, and my husband told me he had forgotten the keys. Jesus always knows your deepest desires. I asked my husband to buy me a CD player and to bring my gospel music. I know Jesus brought them back to me, and I thank Jesus for loving me so much.

When my husband came back, I had my CD player and my music. I was so excited and could not wait to hear the music and rest in His presence. I was so tired of staying at the hospital and wanted to go home so badly. It was so lonely in that room, but while I was in the hospital, Jesus was showing me His word and speaking to me. I understood every word and felt His presence in that room. I was not alone. He was in that room with me, comforting and keeping me safe. I prayed to the Lord and told Him I wanted to go home, but I was not meant to go home at that time. It was a time for the Lord to work and speak to me, to give me strength in faith.

Notes

Notes

Chapter 4

For it is with your heart that you believe and are justified, and it
Is with your mouth that you confess and are saved.
—Rom. 10:10NIV

Jesus knows when we need encouragement. He sent a woman who had breast cancer and had been free from it for twenty years. I did speak to her about Jesus, and now that I think about it, Jesus surely brought her to that room to hear about Him. Jesus is so awesome. Not only did He take care of me, but He was reaching out to her as well. Jesus is no respecter of persons. He loves us each the same, with no favoritism. We are all precious in His sight. Jesus sees us with eyes of love, no matter what we did in the past or what we may do now. He sees us with love and knows that you are precious in His sight. So why would we want to sadden our Lord and Savior?

Repent and let go of all the hurts and pain. Know that Jesus sees you with love in His eyes. You are worthy of His loving embrace and His presence. Let Him wrap His arms around you.

I have to explain to you how the Lord moved in this. I was in the area in the hospital where women give birth. She was an older woman who wasn't pregnant. She was having a test done. She asked me questions, and I told her about Jesus and about how He was telling me I had to do chemotherapy. I remember telling her that Jesus would give me the hair I most desired. She told me about a friend who had beautiful hair after chemotherapy and said that she was doing great. The nurses even asked her if she was sure that she wanted to share a room with me. They told her that I was American and explained what I was going through. She said that she did not have a problem with that, saying that she spoke a little English. It was Jesus' will for her to stay in that room to hear about His love. She was only staying one day. That day, while reading my Bible, a verse popped out at me as if written in bright, bold letters:

With men this is impossible, but with God all things are possible. (Matt. 19:26) NIV

You can just imagine what I was feeling. I knew I had the victory because Jesus was in control. My spirit was filled with joy and was so full of praise I could not help but praise His mighty name. Jesus, what an awesome and mighty God we serve! I knew I was healed, and I thanked Jesus for this. The woman was supposed to go home. I was praying for the Lord to let her stay one more night. Jesus heard that little prayer for His precious daughter and said, "I hear your cry, and because I love you, I will give you your desire." Jesus says that to you; He says, "I am here!"

She came in, and the doctor told her she could go home. She was so happy, and I was sad, but I knew it was not my will but His will be done. Then her husband came in and talked to the doctor, seeing if she could stay one more night. I remember her husband telling me that she could keep me company. Jesus took control and knew my heart. The doctor came in and told her that she had to stay one more night. She was upset but agreed.

That night, Jesus touched me like never before. I had never felt His virtuous healing power as I did on that night. I was listening to my gospel music, and I lifted up my hands and gave it all to Him. Jesus came and grabbed my hands. I felt Him holding them. I let Jesus wrap me in His arms, and everything seemed to disappear. It was just Him and me in that room. I felt as if I were floating on clouds. His touch healed my soul, body, and spirit!

I imagined the women with the twelve blood disease (Mark 5:24-34). Close your eyes and picture that woman who went to every doctor, spending all the money she had to be healed and set free from the disease. Can you imagine? Every time she tried something different, hoping this was it, she still had the same disappointment. Then she heard of Jesus and thought that if she could just touch the hem of His garment, perhaps she would be made whole! I pictured her squeezing through the crowd. She must have been getting bumped into and people are all over, pressing through the crowd to reach her Savior. Maybe she was even thinking, *Will I ever get to Jesus?* Yet she did not give up. She pressed forward, and as she fell to the ground and squeezed her way through, she reached out and touched the hem of His garment. The power that came from Jesus was so strong that it must have felt like fire shooting into her bones.

Even though many people were around Jesus, He stopped and said, "Who touched me?" Jesus felt the power from that one touch. Can you hear His voice? *Who touched me?* There she was on the ground, crying and full of joy, knowing that she was healed. She said, "I touched you," and Jesus turned to her and said, "Daughter, your faith has made you whole!" I love that scripture. It is so romantic and so like our Savior, in that He just reaches out and touches us and everything seems to disappear, leaving just Jesus and us.

I do not know what that woman in Germany must have thought. She was on the other side. So I prayed that He touched her like never before that night. Jesus is worthy of being praised, honored, and glorified! All along, I thought I needed that woman, but now I know that all I need is Jesus. Do not look to people—look to Jesus. He is the one who can guide and direct you into His word, His love, and His presence. When she left the next day, I realized that she hadn't been there to keep me safe, as I'd thought, but that Jesus had more plans than I realized. Now I know that Jesus wanted her to see how it was to know Jesus and to have a peace that nothing could give but Him.

There was one night when I woke up gasping for air, like something or someone was choking me. I started to pray. I know that it was just demonic spirits attacking me, but I was covered with the blood of Jesus. After that night, I slept with my gospel music on and kept my Bible right next to me in bed so I would have my armor of protection.

A final word: be strong with the Lord's mighty power. Put on all God's armor so that you will be able to stand firm against all strategies and tricks of the devil. We are not fighting against people made of flesh and blood but against the evil ruler and authorities of the unseen world, against those mighty powers of darkness who rule this world, and against wicked spirits in the heavenly realms. Use every piece of God's armor to resist the enemy in the time of evil, so that after the battle, you will still be standing firm. Stand your ground, putting on the sturdy belt of truth and the body armor of God's righteousness. For shoes, put on the peace that comes from the good news so that you will be fully prepared. In every battle, you will need faith as your shield to stop all the fiery arrows aimed at you by Satan. Put on salvation as your helmet and take the sword of the Spirit, which is the word of God. Pray at all times and on every occasion in the power of the Holy Spirit. Stay alert and be persistent in your prayers for all Christians everywhere. (Eph. 6:10-18) NIV

As believers in Jesus, we need to be prepared to battle but know that the battle is not ours. It is the Lord's, and as long as we have Jesus on our side, we have the victory! Jesus is preparing His soldiers, gathering them together to show His glory. Everything we go through, the trials and tribulations, is all for His glory and honor, for the enemy is under our feet. In Jesus' name!

Notes

_____

_____

_____

_____

_____

_____

_____

_____

_____

_____

_____

_____

_____

_____

_____

_____

_____

_____

_____

_____

_____

_____

_____

_____

_____

_____

_____

_____

_____

_____

_____

_____

_____

Notes

Chapter 5

The word nourishes our bones and brings
health to your body.
—Prov. 3:8KJV

The top part of my arm was extremely numb, and I had two drains: one for my armpit and one for my breast. It was very uncomfortable, and a nurse would come in to give me a massage with beautifully scented oil. It was so relaxing. One night when giving me a massage, she started talking to me. I knew something was not right as soon as she began telling me it was good to be positive, but that it was very serious because of my age. She said I should get breast cancer books and read them. I was thinking, *No, not breast cancer books*—only Jesus! The authors who wrote those books would not be the ones to heal me. I only know of one healer, and His name is Jesus, Jehovah Rapha the Healer! I did try to read those books, but all they brought was fear and doubt, and the Lord would tell me, "What are you doing? You do not need that. You need my word." The word was what manifested in the healing. I read His word. I slept in His word. I would wake up some nights saying certain scriptures. It was in my spirit.

So if you were to ask me about all that medical terminology, I couldn't say a thing. However, I can say that I have the best thing there is: Jesus my healer. I can tell you about His word on healing, that He is a healer yesterday, today, and forever!

When the nurse left my room, I was so upset that I called my husband and told him what she had said (in addition to the fact that my drains would not come out the next day). My husband told me that she does not believe as we do. I came to find out later that the reason she was like that was because she'd lost someone dear to her the previous year and had therefore lost faith. I pray that Jesus touched her heart and set her free! That night I prayed and told Jesus that I surrender it all to Him, asking him to take control.

I fell asleep listening to "Alabaster Box." Jesus woke me up at 3:37 a.m., during this lyric of the song: "Until the day when Jesus came to me and healed my soul." Jesus not only healed my body; He healed my soul as well. He made me whole that night. Jesus was letting me know that everything was all right! The next morning, a different nurse came in and looked at my drains. Then the doctor came in and said it was okay to remove them. Hallelujah! Jesus healed and restored my body when I surrendered to Him. I gave it to Him, and He took complete control. Sometimes we just need to trust in Jesus and know that all things are possible for our Savior. No man can predict what will happen next. It is all in Jesus' hands. Stop looking to men for the answers. Look to Jesus!

> *For he knoweth not that which shall be: for who can tell him when it shall be? There is no man that hath power over the spirit to retain the spirit; neither hath he power in the day of death: and there is no discharge in that war; neither shall wickedness deliver those that are given to it.* (Ecc. 8:7-8) KJV

I was so excited, for I knew that Jesus was already working and taking over. Full of faith, I was able to take a shower. While I was showering, the enemy started to mess with my mind, and I started looking at my breast differently—not like a breast but a weapon. I started feeling so insecure. But I quickly stopped myself and said that the devil is a liar, and that I would come against those lies in Jesus' name. The most important thing was that I was healed. My breasts were not weapons, and I respected my body. I now realized that God blesses us with beautiful bodies to cherish.

> *But the very hairs of your head are all numbered.* (Matt. 10:30) KJV

They may not be perfect in our sight, but God does not make any mistakes. He made us just the way we are for a reason. I went back to my room and started to read my word and worship His holy name, thanking Jesus for healing me and setting me free.

The doctors came in the next day with the results. While they were speaking to me, the Lord gave me a peace that was unexplainable; it flowed like a river.

> *For thus saith the Lord, Behold, I will extend peace to her like a river, and the glory of the Gentiles like a flowing stream: then shall ye suck, ye shall be borne upon her sides, and be dandled upon her knees. As one whom his mother comforteth, so I will comfort you; and ye shall be comforted in Jerusalem.* (Isa. 66:12-13) KJV

The Lord embraced me in His arms and kept me safe. I must have had a smile on my face while they were telling me, and they must have thought I was crazy. The doctors told me they had removed twenty-three lymph nodes—and nineteen had cancerous cells. Now, you would think I would have been going crazy and crying. But all I could do was rejoice because I knew that Jesus had healed me and set me free from all sickness. They looked at me and asked if I understood how serious it was, and I said yes, but I knew I was healed. The doctors thought I was in denial. They said I would have to get more tests done, and that they would need to test my bones the following day.

As soon as they left, I called my mom, and she told me that the Lord told her to wake up and pray for me. Not only did Jesus give me peace but he did the same for my mother. She worries about everything, but when I told her what had happened, she was calm, and I did not hear any worry in her voice. When Jesus heals you, He lets everyone know that he did so.

> *God is not a man, that he should lie, nor a son of man, that he should repent. Has He said, and will he not do? Or has he spoken, and will he not make it good?* (Num. 23:19) NKJV

Jesus is awesome and mighty when He does something. He is not a man who lies. Jesus is a healer, and I am a standing and walking testimony of that. The Lord told me that I am a walking testimony and that He will never leave me nor forsake me. Jesus is worthy to be praised and worshiped. I feel like jumping and praising His wonderful name. Thank you, Jesus! Don't get me wrong: I still had to fight with my flesh. The enemy would come in like a flood.

I started to think about the bone test and felt I just couldn't hear any more bad results. I did not want to see tests or doctors ever again. When you receive a bad report, you just want to hide and never go to the doctor again. When the enemy comes in like a flood, that is when you need to get your sword out and start reading the word of God. As I was reading my Bible, I looked up 2 Corinthians 1:24. The scripture touched me and gave me peace. The Lord was telling me that He would not give me any bad reports to trouble me.

> *Not for that we have dominion over your faith, but are helpers of your joy: for by faith ye stand.* (2 Cor. 1:24) KJV

When I read that, I started to cry. Jesus knew what I was thinking. I was terrified of the results, and He let me know everything was good news. I went to get my bones checked, and as I lay on that cold, hard bench, I was singing and repeating the verse repeatedly in my head. I was thanking Jesus for my healing. When the results came back, the doctors said my bones were great. All I could do was thank Jesus!

I went back to my room and praised, danced, and worshipped in that hospital room. I did not care who saw me worshipping my Father; I praised Him in that room. I knew I was set free and healed by the blood of Jesus! I am sure that any nurses who may have seen me dancing must have thought that I was in denial, but in the backs of their minds, they must have been saying, *Who is this Jesus that she talks about that healed her?* They had to know that I was not in denial, because Jesus' presence was in that room, and when He shows up, you know He is there. Even ones that do not know Him can feel something as the spirit leaps.

Every time I got over one test report, the enemy always came in to test me again. The doctors came back and told me that I would need chemotherapy and radiation, as well as a five-year treatment plan; however, I was thinking that Jesus has something different in store. Later on that day, the doctors said I would not need the five-year treatment plan. I was very glad, as I wanted to have more children, and I was not getting any younger. I knew the Lord would bless us with two additional children in due time. I could not wait to hold them in my arms and look into their faces, knowing that they were our gift from Jesus.

The doctors told me it would not be easy; the chemotherapy would be strong. They needed to give me three strong, three medium, and three light courses. One of the strongest chemotherapy drugs was called the Red Devil in the States. But I knew whom I served. Jesus was in control, and He would show up and show all. Again, Jesus had different plans. I knew I would get stronger in faith, and when I took the chemotherapy, Jesus would give me a strength that people would not understand. They would be amazed and in awe.

The doctors could not understand why I was not scared, but I had peace. I knew Jesus was in control. He took away all my fears about the treatments and tests that I had to take. I would just be reminded of the scriptures that Jesus placed in my heart and spirit. When I woke up the next day, they came in and told me I would need more tests on my heart and liver. I remembered what Jesus had told me about no more painful visits. I remembered going into those rooms and looking at everyone waiting there. They looked so sad and defeated. I watched how Jesus was working in my life and knew that it was not me but Jesus. I went in to have the test done, and every result came out great. When I got my results, I would say thank you to Jesus, not caring who heard. They would look at me as if I were crazy, but I knew that I was healed, and that they would see Jesus' glory through this trial. All for Jesus' glory!

When the Lord wants you to know something, He will use anyone or anything to get His word out. My brother said something incredible. He said that I would go through the chemotherapy experience to make my testimony stronger. Jesus is in control.

Notes

_____
_____
_____
_____
_____
_____
_____
_____
_____
_____
_____
_____
_____
_____
_____
_____
_____
_____
_____
_____
_____
_____
_____
_____
_____
_____
_____
_____
_____
_____
_____
_____
_____

Notes

_____
_____
_____
_____
_____
_____
_____
_____
_____
_____
_____
_____
_____
_____
_____
_____
_____
_____
_____
_____
_____
_____
_____
_____
_____
_____
_____
_____
_____
_____
_____
_____
_____

Chapter 6

They shall take up serpents; and if they drink any deadly thing,
it shall not hurt them; they shall lay hands on the sick,
and they shall recover.
—Mark 16:18KJV

The Lord said that this sickness was not to harm me but to purify me. Whatever was invading my body, Jesus would take it right out. That which the devil meant for evil, God turned it for my good! Trust in the Lord and know that He will never leave you nor forsake you. No poison will do you harm, and He will give you strength to overcome every side effect. Jesus is going to show up and show all, and all will know that Jesus is the one who healed and restored me. He can do the same for you. Trust in the Lord and He will get you through. Jesus is no respecter person; what He does for one, He will do for you.

> *For there is no respect of persons with God. (Rom. 2:11) KJV*

Sometimes things happen in life that we may not understand, and we need to trust in Jesus and know that He knows what He is doing. No matter what is going on in your life, Jesus will give you the answers you need.

Jesus is knocking at your door and waiting for you to answer. Let Him in; do not push Him away. Jesus wants to embrace you in His mighty arms and love you.

Another day had come, and I woke up anxious. I knew that I was getting ready to go home. I was excited but also nervous because I had to get more tests done. I needed to get my lungs checked. I knew Jesus had healed me and restored me, yet the enemy would come in and test me. I would just quote scriptures, worship His Holy name, and pray. There were days when I felt down, but Jesus always lifted me up and strengthened me like an eagle.

> *He giveth power to the faint; and to them that have no might he increaseth strength. Even the youths shall faint and be weary, and the young men shall utterly fall: but they that wait upon the Lord shall renew their strength; they shall mount up with wings as eagles; they shall run and not be weary; and they shall walk, and not faint. (Isa. 40:29-31) KJV*

The nurse who didn't believe began opening up to me more and saying positive things! It was Jesus; I'd prayed that Jesus would touch her heart and anything that was not of Him she would not be able to speak it, but only speak life. I had the last test for my lungs, and the same nurse who had given me a hard time came in with the results. She said that my lungs were clear and healthy. Hallelujah—all glory and honor unto Jesus! I was so excited and said, "Thank you, Jesus." She smiled, and when I saw her again, she told me she went to church. I was so happy for her, and I was excited that Jesus had touched her. I believe that Jesus healed her heart in His name. Jesus is so awesome! He was taking care of everything. I know my Father was telling me that He would not forsake me, and that I was to trust in Him. I felt Him and could hear Him talking to me. I was so honored that I went through such changes. I would not have changed it for the world. It was the best feeling one could ever have. My Father knows how much I can handle. He knows how much you can handle. All He wants you to do is praise His name and know that He will get you through.

Trust in the Lord with all my heart and lean not on your own understanding; in all your ways acknowledge him, and he will make your paths straight. (Prov. 3:5-6) NIV

I was finally able to go home. I knew they were getting ready for me to try on wigs. I was not excited about that. I was wondering what my husband would think, feeling that everyone was going to look at me differently. I was already insecure about myself and knowing I was going to be bald. I was upset, but then Jesus came and embraced me in His arms. All my fears and burdens disappeared; that is how Jesus is. He comes when everything seems to be falling apart. I realized that Jesus was going to give me the hair I desired most. And Jesus did! He gave me my desired hair. Glory be to God!

I tried on many wigs, all styles and colors. I finally picked a medium-length style but could not stand wearing it because it was so uncomfortable. They showed me how to wash the wig and how to comb it. What an experience. Do I still have that wig? *No!* I am healed and no longer have to wear that wig. Thank you, Jesus!

After that, I went home and stepped inside my prayer closet. I remembered the doctors telling me that my left arm would not be the same again. They said that my arm could swell, and I would have to go in to get it drained. It would be weak, and I would have numbness in my arm because of the number of lymph nodes removed. I started to pray and ask Jesus to heal my left arm and make it just like my right arm. I raised my hands and instantly my left arm started to shake. I felt His virtuous power flow through my left arm, and I was healed. The numbness started to leave, and I felt nervous. It felt like sparks in my arm. Now I have no problems with my left arm. I was made whole. When Jesus does something, He does it completely—not halfway but all the way. He makes no mistakes!

Have faith in God, Jesus answered. I tell you the truth, if anyone says to this mountain. 'Go, throw yourself into the sea,' and does not doubt in his heart but believes that what he says will happen, it will be done for him. Therefore I tell you, whatever you ask for in prayer, believe that you have received it, and it will be yours. And when you stand praying, if you hold anything against anyone, forgive him, so that your Father in heaven may forgive you your sins. (Mark 11:22-25) NIV

The Lord says all you need is just as big as a mustard seed; Jesus is the mighty prince of peace.

I finally found out how long I would have to take chemotherapy and radiation. I would have radiation for one month. When I told my mother, she wanted me to go back to the States. I did not want my husband to see me go through this, so I was really thinking about it going back to the States. See how doubt can creep in? That is why we need to know who we serve and keep ourselves in the word. We need to fight back with God's word because His word fights off demons. The enemy can't stand to hear the word, as the word is stronger than anything.

For the weapons of our warfare are not carnal, but mighty through God to the pulling down of strong holds; casting down imaginations, and every high thing that exalteth itself against the knowledge of God, and bringing into captivity every thought to the obedience of Christ. (2 Cor. 10:4-5) KJV

The enemy comes in and tries to discourage us by using our minds, but we can fight the enemy with the word of God—by standing on His word. When I was praying, the Lord dropped something in my spirit, and it was as if my ears were spiritually open. I started remembering things the enemy said, and I could not help but say, "Wow, the enemy twists the word!" The enemy brings fear and confusion, and the Lord was letting me know when the enemy was talking. When Jesus speaks, He gives you peace and a sound mind. Jesus does not do anything in vain; He brings everything together and takes complete control. I had my up and downs, and the Lord always confirmed His word to me.

Once when I was cooking dinner and listening to music, the enemy was attacking my mind. I just wanted to scream and give up. I felt as if a big dump truck were on top of me. I felt so overwhelmed. I heard the CD turn off, so I went to try to put the song back to where it had been. The CD would not change, so I realized that maybe the Lord wanted me to hear the song. I let it play. I stopped everything I was doing as I heard the song saying the storm was over. I started to cry and praise His name, worshipping Him in that room. I lifted my hands in the air and felt a release, just as I did when I heard that song. I felt light as a feather. Hallelujah! When the song was over, I was able to get the CD to scan to the next songs. Jesus is good.

Notes

Notes

Chapter 7

Surely he will save you from the fowler's snare
and from the deadly pestilence.
—Ps. 91:3NIV

The next journey began when I started the chemotherapy treatments. I didn't know what to expect. I always prayed to my Father, and he gave me a scripture:

And he said unto them, Go ye into all the world, and preach the gospel to every creature. He that believeth and is baptized shall be saved; but he that believeth not shall be damned. And these signs shall follow them that believe; in my name shall they cast out devils; they shall speak with new tongues; they shall take up serpents; and if they drink any deadly thing, it shall not hurt them; they shall lay hands on the sick, and they shall recover. (Mark 16:15-18) KJV

I knew that Jesus was with me, and that whatever was coming in, He was going to take right out. It would not harm me. My faith grew, and I trusted Jesus. No poison from the chemotherapy was going to harm me, for God was on my side. I went to the hospital and was listening to my gospel music and praising Jesus. I was waiting for them to start the injection. For the first treatment, I remember seeing a bag. It was red, and I could smell it, though that may sound strange. I started to see the chemotherapy treatment going through the tube, and I could feel it coming into my body. I felt I had no control, but I knew that Jesus was with me and in control. I started to pray and instantly it went away. I was sitting on the bed, listening to the music, meditating on the word, and keeping my focus on the Lord. I was there for a long time, and when it was finished, I felt light-headed and a little nauseated. I went to the bathroom, praying to the Lord to take this feeling away. When I came out of the restroom, I felt better. I trusted and believed that Jesus could take everything that I felt and melt it all away. The nurses were amazed about how I'd done, so I told them it was Jesus!

When I went home, my husband left to get us something to eat. I had a craving for vegetables, which I had never liked, so I knew that was Jesus. Then I started to feel my body ache all over. I went to the prayer room and started to read my word and pray. I tried to go to sleep but I could not. I started to cry and to pray to Jesus, asking Him to please take the pain away and let me sleep in peace. Instantly the pain was gone, and I had peace. I started to cry and ask Jesus why we doubt Him! Jesus does so much for us. He told me that He would never leave me nor forsake me. Jesus gave me strength every day.

I had many churches praying for me, and I remember that while I was sleeping that night, I woke up because I heard someone speaking in tongues, praying. I knew it was someone praying for me; you can feel saints praying. I thank everyone who prayed and lifted my family and me up in prayer, for prayer is a mighty weapon. You can do a lot through prayer. Do not ever stop speaking to Jesus, because through prayer, breakthroughs come. Look at me. I am a walking testimony of those prayers. Jesus gave me strength and healed me. I am so grateful. Writing this reminds me of what I felt during those days when taking the chemotherapy, and I thank God I no longer have to do that. The Lord said to me, "As the sky is forever blue, you are forever healed!" Each time I went in for a treatment, I would feel Jesus's presence embracing me and giving me a strength that was unexplainable.

Once when I was in the hospital receiving a treatment, I was walking down the hall and glancing in the rooms. I told the Lord that the people looked so sad, and there was so much darkness. It was like looking at a gloomy picture. The enemy held the emotions in bondage. I started to pray for them, and it touched me because it showed that Jesus was with me. I could not have done it without Jesus. As a nation, we need to get back to praising Jesus rather than ourselves. We have become so self-righteous. You did not wake yourselves up. Jesus was the one who got you up this morning. Repent and ask God for forgiveness, for we are nothing without Jesus!

People ask me how I did it, and I tell them it was Jesus. If it had been me, I wouldn't have gotten through. The enemy would have held me in bondage. Jesus gets us through everyday life.

Jesus gave me cravings for healthy food, and I was constantly hungry throughout those treatments. My hair started to fall out during the second treatment. I was not upset, and I told my mom to shave it off. It felt good just to get it all off at once. There were days when my entire body ached terribly, and I would soak in a hot bath and pray. Jesus always saved me and gave me strength. I felt better every day that I got stronger in faith. Jesus gave me strength. Jesus showed me the following scripture:

For David speaketh concerning him, I forsaw the Lord always before my face, for he is on my right hand, that I should not be moved: therefore did my heart rejoice, and my tongue was glad; more over also my flesh shall rest in hope; because thou wilt not leave my soul in hell, neither wilt thou suffer thine Holy one to see corruption. Thou hast made known to me the ways of life; thou shalt make me full of joy with thy countenance. (Acts 2:25-28) KJV

Jesus answered and said unto him, If a man love him, and we will come unto him, and make our abode with him. He that loveth me not keepeth not my sayings: and the word which ye hear is not mine, but the Father's which sent me. These things have I spoken unto you, being yet present with you. But the Comforter, which is the Holy Ghost, whom the Father will send in my name, he shall teach you all things, and bring all things to your remembrance whatsoever I have said unto you. Peace I leave with you, my peace I give unto you: not as the world giveth, give I unto you. Let not your heart be troubled, neither let it be afraid. (John 14:23-27) KJV

Jesus would remind me of His peace and know that this is it—that it is finished. The blood of Jesus has healed me. It is written in red!

Each day I went in for a treatment, my faith grew. When it finally came to the weakest chemotherapy, I was thinking, *Yes, this will be nothing.* But the weakest chemotherapy drugs make you unable to empty your bladder. You have to take pills to make your bladder work. I would feel all the chemotherapy sitting in my stomach. It was so disgusting. If you remember, Jesus said that everything coming in, He was taking it out. That is exactly what He did. It came out; it did not stay in my body. I thank Jesus for keeping His word.

I was already without hair, and I did not wear my wig very much. I did not like wearing it at all. I remember being so excited when my hair started to grow back. When I had enough hair to start wearing it without a wig, I was afraid. I always had long hair and did not want anybody to see me with short hair. I remember going to a women's ministry and taking off the wig. I had the peace to wear my hair short, and I felt so free! When I was going through the chemotherapy treatments, losing my hair was hard. But I remember asking the Lord to give me back beautiful curly hair, and the Lord gave me the beautiful hair my heart had desired. I always thought I wanted my hair straight before I went through all this, but I realized that God gave me curly hair for a reason.

God made me, and I am not insecure about having a few scars. I look at my battle scars and realize that those are my reminders of where Jesus has brought me from. Those scars keep me in line when I go through trials and tribulations. When I feel I can't make it another day, my Father steps in and reminds me of what He has brought me from, and I press on in

Jesus' name. When I was in the hospital, the Lord told me He was preparing His soldiers. That is what Jesus is doing: getting His soldiers ready to battle in Jesus' name. Seek His word and embrace yourself in His presence.

> *And Jesus said unto them, I am the bread of life: he that cometh to me shall never hunger; and he that believeth on me shall never thirst. But I said unto you, that ye also have seen me, and believe not. All that the Father giveth me shall come to me; and him that cometh to me I will in no wise cast out. For I came down from heaven, not to do mine own will, but the will of him that sent me. And this is the Father's will which hath sent me, that of all which he hath given me I should lose nothing, but should raise it up again at the last day. And this is the will of him that sent me, that every one which seeth the Son, and believeth on him may have everlasting life: and I will raise him up at the last day.* (John 6:35-40) KJV

Notes

Notes

_____
_____
_____
_____
_____
_____
_____
_____
_____
_____
_____
_____
_____
_____
_____
_____
_____
_____
_____
_____
_____
_____
_____
_____
_____
_____
_____
_____
_____
_____
_____
_____

Chapter 8

For to me, to live is Christ, and to die is gain
(Philippians 1:21) NIV

When we go through trials and tribulations, it is not to defeat us but to make us, for it is all for Jesus' glory. We have the victory!

And he said unto me, My grace is sufficient for thee: for my strength is made perfect in weakness. Most gladly therefore will I rather glory in my infirmities, the power of Christ may rest upon me. Therefore I take pleasure in infirmities, in reproaches, in necessities, in persecutions, in distresses for Christ's sake: for when I am weak, then am I strong.
(2 Cor. 12:9-10) KJV

When I went through this trial, Jesus gave me the strength to go through chemotherapy and radiation. The doctors were astonished and in awe of what Jesus did for me. He can and will do for you if you trust in His word. When Jesus says something is done, it is finished. There is no going back on His word. I am not saying that it was all easy, but I know that when I called on the name of Jesus, all my enemies had to flee in Jesus' name. Now here I am, writing this book for Jesus, and I have the victory. The blood of Jesus has healed me. Hold on to His garment and do not let go. There is so much more to Jesus and so much more to learn. Jesus will open doors that you could never imagine, showing you things to come that you will not believe!

I remember the Lord telling me that he was not finished with me yet, telling me that I would go through more trials and tribulations. I know He would never leave me nor forsake me. If Jesus got me through this trial and healed me, what couldn't my Father do?

I was telling a TRICARE regional office that I had a vision about sharing the testimony with short curly hair in front of people. They looked at me as if I were crazy. When they see me, they are in awe of Jesus' mighty hand. I had a difficult time accepting that I had to get radiation, so I prayed and fasted, knowing I was healed. I did not understand why I had to do this.

Toward the end of the chemotherapy, I'd had enough. I did not want to go through the radiation. I told Jesus that I did not want to do it, but I said that if it was his will, I would do it to bring glory to his name. That night, I went to prayer service, and while I was praying, Jesus told me that my sickness was not to harm me but to purify me. I knew then that I had to go through with the radiation.

I went to see the doctor the next day. Before I left, I was reading the word and kept seeing "Fear not; I am with thee." When I got to the hospital to talk to them, they explained the side effects, and I was intimidated. I did not want to sign that paper. I remember looking at it and asking Jesus if I had to. I knew what the Lord had said, and I had to trust in Him with all my heart. I knew that He would not let any harm come to me. The Holy Spirit reminded me of the Lord saying to fear not, that he is with me. That is when I said, "Let's do it." I signed the paper and was not afraid. If Jesus was on my side, who could be against me? I went in for my radiation treatment, and everything was great. There were no complications, of course, as Jesus was with me!

Through all this chemotherapy, the doctors said there was a good chance I would not be able to have any more children. I went to a women's ministry, and as I was praying for at least one more baby, the Lord showed me a scripture, which I will paraphrase. It said that I would not believe if it were told to me. One of the women came up to pray for me, and she said that I would have not just one baby but another, and that the devil was deceiving me so that I would think it would just be one more. Jesus is so awesome and powerful!

One Sunday after church, on February 5, 2006, one of the sisters came up to me and said that the Lord said all the impurities were out of my body, and the healing process had begun. The next day I started my menstrual cycle. It was back to normal, with no complications. The doctors were afraid I was going to get pregnant, but it was all in my Father's hands. He blesses us with the gift of children.

During the radiation, I was having marital problems. My husband and I were on two different paths. He was like a stranger to me, and I was a stranger to him. My husband wanted the old Regina, and I was not going to go back to that Regina ever again. I was going to seek Jesus and do His will. We would argue because he did not want me to go to church. Men bottle up their emotions and we let out our emotions. I did not have my husband to talk to, but I had Jesus. One day I was praying and telling the Lord that if my husband did not want to be with me, I would be all right as long as I had Jesus. He showed me a scripture, and I remember telling Him that I need him to be my husband.

> *For thy Maker is thine husband; the Lord of hosts is his name; and thy Redeemer the Holy One of Israel; The God of the whole earth shall he be called.* (Isa. 54:5) KJV

All I could do was weep and thank Jesus for His word and his promises. I trusted God to work out our marriage. I would go to church and keep praying, asking Jesus to transform my husband like never before. I wanted a complete transformation. I asked the Holy Spirit to hit him like a tsunami. I asked the Lord why this was happening, and He said that first he had to change me, and then he would get to him. I knew we were meant to be together. Jesus brought us together, and nothing could tear us apart. You may ask how I knew he was the one. I remember that when we were dating, I'd pray and ask Jesus if this was the man. I said, "If so, let him propose to me. If not, then let him move on." He proposed to me, and here we are.

Back to how awesome Jesus is and how He knows the plans for us way before we are in our mothers' wombs. My husband and I were still kissing each other good-bye in the mornings. Everything seemed good until I saw something that hurt me badly. I was so angry and said, "This is it, Jesus. I can't take this anymore. I am going to divorce him. I'm done with him." When I went to church that night, I was so upset and just wanted to cry, but I held back my tears. No one knew what I was going through but Jesus. The pastor stopped the whole service and said, "No one in here is thinking of divorcing." I just started to cry. I was in shock after that, and Jesus gave me His love and compassion. If it had been me, I would have held a grudge, but not Jesus.

When I got home, my husband wanted to talk. I told him how I felt and what I thought of his e-mailing another girl. Upset and with tears in his eye, he said he was sorry. I knew at that moment that Jesus was already working in our relationship. Jesus told me to hug him and tell him I love him and forgive him. I did, and it was awesome. I trust my husband more than ever and know my husband is saved. He is filled with the Holy Ghost. Everything I prayed for was spoken that day. My husband was at the altar, and I was so excited and leaping for joy. Jesus knows the plan He has for us.

Notes

_____

_____

_____

_____

_____

_____

_____

_____

_____

_____

_____

_____

_____

_____

_____

_____

_____

_____

_____

_____

_____

_____

_____

_____

_____

_____

_____

_____

_____

_____

_____

_____

_____

Notes

Chapter 9

For I know the thoughts that I think toward you,
saith the Lord, thoughts of peace, and not of evil,
to give you an expected end.
—Jer. 29:11KJV

Jesus knows the plan He has for us. He has it all planned out. He knew our plans before we were in our mothers' wombs. My husband was in school in Fort Hood, and he was supposed to go to school for his staff sergeant rank for the military. He was supposed to go to school sooner, but for reasons we know now, his school date was pushed to a different date. If my husband had gone when he was supposed to, he would never have meet Brother Patrick. Brother Patrick was stationed in Germany, and because of his obedience to the voice of God, he saved two lost souls and then some. It would be passed down from generation to generation. So do not miss out on being obedient to the voice of God. When He says do it, just do it! You may feel that your voice is not being heard, but believe me when I say that Jesus is keeping everything in His record. So do not give up and do not give in.

I can look back and remember all the people who bore witness to me. Some spoke to me about Jesus. There was one in particular who lived the life of a follower of Jesus. I can remember her as if it were yesterday. I was working for a bank, and the woman always had a smile on her face, a radiant glow. She never let anything get her down. She may have not known she was witnessing, but she was and still is to this day. I remember her and thank her so much for just living the word. She was truly a virtuous woman! I can remember another woman at my job who was saved and Jesus healed her marriage. I thought these people were crazy, but they impacted my life so much. We never know how we may impact someone's life, but we are definitely depositing seeds into lives.

My husband's friend told him about IWC, a church in Germany. That's where I met my spiritual parents. I thank the Lord for them. They taught us how to know Jesus personally and changed our lives to seek His face. They taught us what a Christian is by living the word daily. The Lord will lead you to your spiritual parents. They will teach and raise you up for that season. I was already searching for Jesus, and Jesus was already calling me to the kingdom.

We tried everything to avoid having to go to Germany, but nothing worked. In fact, they even said if my husband did not go, he would be kicked out of the military. That was not going to happen; my husband was a soldier and loved the military. So we decided to go to Germany. We got the dates for the movers and started looking on the Internet at where we were going, which was Hanau, Germany. As you know, God will not force us. At the very end, they said, "If you do not want to go, we will send you to El Paso." But we had already set the dates for the trip and had everything already in place, and at that point, we wanted to go to Germany. We were excited and could not wait. It is something how God knows the plans He has for us.

The funny thing is, when we were in Houston saying good-bye to everyone, I told my sister-in-law that I felt God had something for me. I did not know what it was, but I had always felt that it was a small voice saying, "This is the way—walk." I had no idea that this was the journey to open doors, and I can't help but praise His Holy name. *Jesus* . . . Just say that beautiful name with me. *Jesus!* There is power in the name Jesus! He is worthy to be praised! As I am writing this, I feel His presence. His anointing embrace. His loving embrace. Jesus is not finished with you yet; it is just the beginning. Trust in Him. Don't try to understand. Just trust. Let go and fall into His arms. Know that God is on your side. He will show you things that you will not believe. I felt that Jesus was holding me and letting me know that in due time I would understand everything that was going on. He will never leave you nor forsake you. Jesus works in mysterious ways.

> *For my thoughts are not your thoughts, neither are your ways my ways, saith the Lord.*
> (Isa. 55:8) KJV

He brings people onto your path to help you, but little do you know that you are helping them through their problems as well. For example, when my sister-in-law and I talked, she would help me in so many ways. She told me one day that I had been helping her to heal her insecurities, yet she had been helping me with my own insecurities at the same time. There were days when I would wake up and fear falling down, but the Lord always lifted me up in my time of need. Consider these two scriptures:

> *Be still before the LORD and wait patiently for him; do not fret when people succeed in their ways, when they carry out their wicked schemes.* (Ps. 37:7) NIV

> *Fear thou not; for I am with thee: be not dismayed; for I am thy God: I will strengthen thee; yea, I will help thee; yea, I will uphold thee with the right hand of my righteousness.* (Isa. 41:10) KJV

With Him, all things are possible. Jesus will take care of everything so enjoy every single day. For this is the day that Jesus made for you!

I remember walking through my house, putting some things away and wondering if I would see my son grow up to be a man. Also, would I have more children? That day, the enemy was attacking my mind. I have photographs of my family on the wall of my hallway, and as I walked by, the Lord told me to go back and look at the photographs. He said that I was going to have many photos on the wall. I started crying and praising His Holy name. I felt His presence in that place and a peace that overflowed my life. Jesus is so awesome and mighty, and you know that Jesus always confirms what He says.

Notes

_____
_____
_____
_____
_____
_____
_____
_____
_____
_____
_____
_____
_____
_____
_____
_____
_____
_____
_____
_____
_____
_____
_____
_____
_____
_____
_____
_____
_____
_____

Notes

Chapter 10

*So I will restore to you the years that the swarming locust has eaten
the crawling locust, the consuming locust, and the chewing locust,
my great army which I sent among you.*
—Joel 2:25NKJV

I was using a woman's car because ours broke down. When I took the car back, I did not know Jesus was going to speak to me through her. She said, "God told me that you are going to have one child, and right after that, you will have another. She also told me that I will have many photos on the wall!" See how awesome He is. Jesus will always confirm His word. Before she told me that, I would always tell my husband that I felt we were going to have another child. Of course, I knew this because God was speaking to me about our babies.

I was reading my journal and looking over everything that I had written down, and I read something so awesome. It was the Lord speaking to me; I had written that the Lord had something better for us as a family. *I see you working so much, and I just praise and glorify your name, Jesus. Thank you, my heavenly Father, for you have brought good sisters and brothers to us.* I prayed that when people looked at me, they would see victory, not defeat. Everybody at IWC saw victory. *Thank you, heavenly Father. I know there is so much to come, so many gifts that even are more amazing! I have overcome this!* The Lord speaks to us in so many ways, and we do not notice.

My husband loves the Lord as much as I do. We put Jesus first above everything else. Jesus is worthy of being praised and honored. Jesus saved my husband and brought our relationship back together. My son David loves Jesus, and I will bring my children up to serve the Lord.

One day in September 2007, I was going to the gym to work out. I was listening to my iPod, and a song about testimonies came on. Listening to the words, I realized what a pretty song it was. It reminded me of when God said I was a walking testimony. The Lord always reminds you what He has in store for you.

When I went to make another appointment for my three-month checkup, I saw this young German man. He must have been about twenty, and he knew me from when I had come out of my surgery three years previously. Full of joy, I asked him how he was doing. He said that he did not recognize me, and that every time he saw me, he forgot all his problems. He asked me how I did it, and I said that it was Jesus. The best thing I heard was when he said that it made him believe in Jesus. I wanted to shout and speak in tongues, but I would have scared him. It made me see that God was shining His light through me, even if I felt I wasn't worthy. He chose me to bring glory to His name. I realized at that time that every time I went for my checkups, it was not for me but for them to see Jesus. I know that those doctors, in the backs of their minds, were saying what that young man said. Jesus is worthy of being praised! I remember listening to a song about God shining the moon on you. Think about a full moon, how it is big and bright. It warms your heart. That's a little like God's love. It is so much more than that, but He shows us through His creation how much He loves us. He also says it in His word:

> *For God so loved the world, that he gave his only begotten Son, that whosoever believeth in him should not perish, but have everlasting life.* (John 3:16) KJV

The Lord woke me up about five o'clock one morning, and when I opened my eyes, there was a big full moon right outside my window. I could not help but cry, knowing that it was a kiss from my Father.

So many of us look to Jesus as a genie in a bottle when things are going bad. But when things are good, we forget all about who set us free. Let us be truthful. I know I used to be that person; I would look for Jesus only when I needed Him, and when I received what I was asking for, I would go right back into the world. It is so sad. I pray that this will change the way you look at our Father. I know that you would not want your children only to come to you when they want something; you would like your child to spend some time with you. That is how our Father feels. He wants that intimate relationship with us. He desires to speak and communicate with His children.

> *And as he entered into a certain village, there met him ten men that were lepers, which stood afar off: and they lifted up their voices, and said Jesus, Master, have mercy on us. And when he saw them, he said unto them, go show yourselves unto the priests, and it came to pass, that, as they went, they were cleansed. And one of them, when he saw that he was healed, turned back and with a loud voice glorified God, and fell down on his face at his feet giving him thanks: and he was a Samaritan. And Jesus answering said, were there not ten cleansed? But where are the nine? There are not found that returned to give glory to God, save this stranger. And he said unto him, Arise, go thy way: thy faith hath made thee whole.* (Luke 17:12-19) KJV

This scripture speaks to every one of us. Jesus cleansed those ten men, yet only one fell on his face to worship at His feet. I can't imagine how Jesus must have felt. Some may say He was angry, but I do not see that, for Jesus has so much love and compassion. He was sad that with the exception of the one man, they did not come back to give God the glory. I know how it is to be healed by the grace of God. Jesus healed and restored me to be whole. I give Him praise in everything that I do and for the uplifting of the kingdom of God.

> *For by grace are ye saved through faith; and that not of yourselves: it is the gift of God.*
> (Eph. 2:8) KJV

Even though I did not know Jesus and ran away from Him, He still called me to the kingdom of God. He still loves me enough to save me and heal and restore me. He loves you so much that He wants to rejoice over you with a song.

> *The Lord thy God in the midst of thee is mighty; he will save, he will rejoice over thee*
> *with joy; he will rest in his love, he will joy over thee with singing.* (Zeph. 3:17) KJV

Notes

_____
_____
_____
_____
_____
_____
_____
_____
_____
_____
_____
_____
_____
_____
_____
_____
_____
_____
_____
_____
_____
_____
_____
_____
_____
_____
_____
_____
_____
_____
_____
_____
_____
_____

Notes

Chapter 11

Come and see the works of God; He is awesome
In His doing toward the sons of men.
—Ps. 66:5NKJV

Do not be one of those ones who did not return to give glory unto our Lord and Savior. Be one who returned to praise and lift up His name. He is worthy of being praised. He loves us so much that we cannot even contain it. We think we know what love is, but until we know intimately who Jesus is, we have no idea. I can't even imagine living my life without Jesus. I did for many years and wonder how I did it—because now that I have Him in my life, I will not go without my Father. He is first in my life, and He is worthy of being praised. I know I mention that a lot, but you have to understand that there are just no words to explain His glorious love and His awesome power. Just say that He is worthy of being praised.

When I was at choir practice, I felt so far away from God. I prayed and asked the Lord to say something, anything. I just needed to hear Him. When I went home, my family and I went out to a German restaurant, and they had music playing. When you walk in, the atmosphere has to change because you are the Father's child. His light shines through you. As we sat down, a song that I love came on. I actually created a dance to the song just for my Father. The Lord is so good and loves us so much! Now, you have to understand that they do not have gospel music playing on the radio in Germany. So as I heard that song, I said, "Ah!" That was my song, and I knew my Father was there. I was so excited, and it made my night—a kiss from the King. Little things like that are so awesome. I am His beloved and so are you!

I was wondering one day about the word "beloved," so I looked in the dictionary. It means dearly loved. What turned my attention to the word was the fact that I was asking the Lord one day what my name was. I know my name is Regina, but you know how Abraham's name was Abram, Isaiah's name was Jacob, and Sarah's name was Sarai? Well, I started wondering what my name was, for I was no longer that same person. I started to pray about it, asking my Father, "What is my name?" If you ask Jesus for anything, even something that sounds silly like this, He will answer because He loves us so much and we are precious in His sight.

One day while I was getting dressed for church, I turned on the church channel, which is what we have here in Germany, and I was watching and listening to the word. All of a sudden, the pastor said, "Your name is beloved." I started to cry and was so excited, but all of us are His beloved. He loves us so much. If we would just grasp that, we would know that no weapon formed against us shall prosper. As I was reading a scripture, it stood out to me like never before—it touched me so much.

> *When I remember thee upon my bed, and meditate on thee in the night watches. Because thou has been my help, therefore in the shadow of thy wings will I rejoice. My soul followeth hard after thee: thy right hand upholdeth me.* (Ps. 63:6-8) KJV

When I think back to how Jesus delivered me and was my help, all I can do is sing with joy, knowing I am under His righteous right arm, protected in His love. I know I can look back at all those years of my life that seemed wasted away and realize it was all for His glory. I know I can rejoice, glorify His name, and meditate on all the things that He saved me from, knowing that I am in His arms.

Do not look back at the past. Look toward the future with your wonderful Father who is in heaven. Know that the past is gone and under the blood and know the future is for His glory. All those testimonies He has given you can be shared. He blessed you by His grace, and it can all be for His glory. Lift up His son Jesus and magnify His name. I know now that the past is done and gone, and I can rejoice knowing that my Father gave me a second chance to live my life. I will not waste my life on the worldly things that will pass away; I know that what I do here is for my Father. It is recorded in the Lamb's book of life. Everything else that I did in the past is washed away. So do not look back but look forward. His presence is guiding and directing you to grow in His love.

Have you ever read the book on Ester and learned how, through faith, she was able to do all that she did? I recommend reading Ester. What a testimony. I wonder what she was thinking and how she felt when she was going through the trial. Yet she held her head high, knowing whom she served. It reminds me of that intimate relationship we have with the Lord. He is our King, and we are precious jewels in His eyes. Ester walked by faith, not by sight, and the Lord kept her safe and in His arms. Even though you are going through this trial, keep your head up knowing that when it is the right time for Jesus, He will pull you out unharmed, into His loving arms. Keep your head up. Do not let the enemy tell you lies. Know whom you serve—an awesome and mighty God!

I was admiring the beautiful day one September morning. When I looked at the clouds, the trees and every colorful flower, I saw God's glory, radiant and shining. I started to think of those who feel life is not worth living. I started to pray: *Lord, open their spiritual eyes that they may see your beauty—how radiant you are and how each and every day they can wake up and praise your name. The trees are glistening against the wind. As the wind blows, it's like a soft breath from you, wrapping me in your arms. You blessed us with heaven and Earth, and we get a little glimpse of your beauty. When we just look through our spiritual eyes, we will see how blessed we are.*

I was thinking about and looking at His creation in complete awe! I told Jesus to remind me of what I had been saying in order to write this book. Again, this is not my book; it is all Jesus'. It is not for me; it is for the next generation. It is for you, the reader. It is to teach us to keep praise on our lips and joy in knowing our salvation, Jesus.

> *Let this be written for a future generation, that a people not yet created may praise the Lord.* (Ps. 102:18) NIV

God sees us with eyes of love, no matter what we did in the past or what we may do now. He sees us with love and knows that you are precious in His sight. You are worthy of His love. Embrace His presence and let Him wrap His arm around you.

Notes

_____
_____
_____
_____
_____
_____
_____
_____
_____
_____
_____
_____
_____
_____
_____
_____
_____
_____
_____
_____
_____
_____
_____
_____
_____
_____
_____
_____
_____

Notes

Chapter 12

It is wonderful to know that all our sins are washed away, never to haunt us again. Some of you may be wondering how I overcome the fear and anxieties I have. All I can say is *Jesus*—seeking His face and trusting in His word. Let me be honest: there were times when I felt so overwhelmed, when I would run to the doctor with every little pain. They would look at me as if I were crazy. I felt crazy. I knew what Jesus had said: "It won't come back. I am your physician." Learning to trust in Jesus and have that patience through the trials of being set free and delivered from all fear was the hard part. You may go through a trial, but it is all for God's glory. I was going through a tough time, and I knew the trial was coming because the Lord told me I was going to go through one.

A couple of weeks later, I saw a demonic spirit grabbing my lower left back. I felt a pull, and I kept running to the doctors, knowing what it was. It was nothing that a doctor could handle. They did not see anything wrong, and they looked at me as if I were crazy. Finally, the Lord told me not to go to the doctor, saying that there was nothing wrong with me. Now don't get me wrong: the Lord was not telling me never to go to the doctor again. No, it was just this one instance; He wanted me to trust in Him. He will always confirm it with someone else, and He did that time as well. I had two sisters who helped me and gave me strength in His word. I thank the Lord for my sisters in Christ.

The Lord also gave me a scripture:

> *In the thirty-ninth year of his reign, Asa developed a serious foot disease. Even when the disease became life threatening, he did not seek the Lord's help but sought help only from his physicians. So he died in the forty-first year of his reign.* (2 Chron. 16:12-13) NLT

It was ordained for me to go through this trial because Jesus knew I had to let go of my fear and trust in Him with all my heart. It was so hard when Jesus said to stand still and know that he is God. I had to put my trust in Jesus to walk in victory! Jesus told me fear not! I AM! Fear not! I AM! If I am for you, who can be against you? No devil in hell. I had to overcome my fear, trust in my Father, and know that He has me in the palm of His hands.

He told me to fast for three days. It was hard at first, and I could only go for a day and a half. Finally, I did it! I fasted for three days and received my breakthrough Jesus confirmed every word! The Lord revealed to me the scripture that He had given me at the beginning:

> *This sickness will not end in death but it will be to glorify my son's name.* (John 11:4) NIV

Just recently, I was asking the Lord about the scripture, and He revealed it to me in different pieces. Now I see that Jesus had my steps ordered the entire time. When they called for Jesus to come and heal Lazarus, he did not come right away. He waited two days. That spoke to me because Jesus could have healed me right away. I would not have had to go through the surgery, chemotherapy, and radiation, but then it would not have glorified Jesus' name. He may not come when we want Him to, but He will show up. The Lord was letting me know that the sickness would not end in death, and that spoke to me. It said that Jesus was going to come right on time, and He did. I was praying, and the Lord told me it was time for me to unravel my grave clothes and live and declare my glory! When I heard that, I realized that Jesus had revealed so much to me in that one scripture. I could not see that then, but the Lord always reveals at the right time. When Jesus called out to Lazarus, he came, and Jesus told him to take off those grave clothes. Lazarus gave all the glory and honor to Jesus. God is omnipresent and worthy of being praised.

It is all about knowing when you need to trust in Jesus. The right relationship means knowing that no weapon formed against you shall prosper. All you need is Jesus! You need healing Jesus! You need a breakthrough in fear, doubt, and anxieties. I knew my Father in all those trials. Jesus came in and set my feet on solid ground. He never left me nor forsook me, and He will be with you all the way. I know now how to fight the enemy. Anytime he comes and tries to lie to me, I will say, "Devil, you are a liar because my Father says that I am healed by the blood of Jesus and it will not come back. He is my physician. No longer do I have to fear. No longer will I be bound in anxiety and doubt, as I have the victory in Jesus's name! My Father has my steps in order. He ordained for me to live and declare Jesus' glory, so whatever He declares, it is settled! For I shall live and declare the glory of the Lord!" Rise up and take your stand. As the royal priesthood, you are not to let any enemy come and lie to you. If God is for you, who can be against you! *You are healed in the name of Jesus!* Let the peace overflow you right now and let Him embrace you in His love!

> *Truly I tell you, whatever you bind on earth will be bound in heaven, and whatever you loose on earth will be loosed in heaven.* (Matt. 18:18) NIV

Arise and walk in the anointing that Jesus has placed on your life! What an honor to be here for Jesus—to be that light to the lost and set the captives free. Glory is to our Savior, Jesus Christ of Nazareth, who is worthy of being praised on mountaintops and through the valleys. Jesus' peace flows like a sparkling river beside the dry land. Jesus is a gently blowing breeze against the trees as the leaves clap to His presence. You can't help but shout hallelujah! Praise to the Almighty God!

It is something how the Lord lets you know Him by many names. For instance, I can say that I know the Lord as Jehovah-Shalom. You can imagine how I reacted when the doctors came in and told me I had breast cancer. The fear tripled inside me; it was a strong bondage. I had nightmares every night. It seemed evil spirits were tormenting me and trying to snatch my life away. I would get myself up and praise and worship His name.

> *And now shall mine head be lifted up above mine enemies round about me; therefore will I offer in his tabernacle sacrifices of joy; I will sing, yea, I will sing praises unto the Lord.* (Ps. 27:6) KJV

Many times, we put on masks to try to hide our thoughts and fears. I was doing a great job of that. I remember when I first went to IWC. As soon as I walked in, I wanted to run to the front and cry at Jesus's feet. I felt His presence and knew He was there. I could picture myself lying at His feet, tears running down my cheeks and Jesus embracing me with His love, letting me know that everything was going to be all right. I cannot imagine how Mary Magdalene felt when she washed Jesus' feet with her tears.

I just have to say the name *Jesus*. I can't say enough how awesome He is. I was struggling, wondering whether the cancer was coming back, and I fought the enemy with praise and worship.

One Sunday I opened my closet, and as soon as I did so, it was like a flood of fear and thoughts coming into my mind. I remember praying and telling the Lord that I couldn't wait until the doctors said it was done. That Sunday at church, I went up for prayer. No one knew what I said in my prayer closet except the Lord and me. Bishop Miller came up to pray with me, and again no one knew. The Lord was speaking to me, saying, "It won't come back. I am your physician so have peace." I started to cry and thank the Lord, for only He knew what I needed to hear.

> *O Lord, thou hast searched me, and known me. Thou knowest my downsitting and mine uprising, thou understandest my thought afar off.* (Ps. 139:1-2) KJV

Jesus, set me free from fear and the Lord said: the enemy can't come to me in that area no more. It has been left at my Father's feet! I can shout Hallelujah! Praise to the Almighty Jehovah! He is the great I AM! There is nothing too hard for our Lord and Savior. I pray that you give all your fears and doubts unto the Lord. Jesus is not a respecter person. If He did it for me, He can do it for you. The Lord keeps His word. He blessed my husband and me with twins, a boy and a girl, and another son. We have been blessed with four healthy and vigorous children sprouting out like olive trees (Ps. 128). When he speaks, it will come to pass. Write the vision and make it plan.

> *For there is no respect of persons with God.* (Rom. 2:11) KJV

Reach out to Jesus and surrender all to Him. Jesus is waiting with His arms wide open, ready to deliver you from all your fears and doubts and to set a standard against the enemy.

> *What is impossible with man is possible with God.* (Luke 18:27) NIV

Lay your burdens at His feet today and rejoice with praise in your heart, knowing that Jesus has set you free. Jesus, I pray for the person reading this testimony. In Jesus' name I pray, amen! Glory be to God!

Notes

Notes

Healing Scriptures

And God wrought special miracles by the hands of Paul: so that from his body were brought unto the sick handkerchiefs or aprons, and the diseases departed from them, and the evil spirits went out of them.
—Acts 19:11-12KJV

I pray that you know Jesus as your personal Savior. If not it is not too late for you. All you have to do is say a prayer and ask Jesus into your heart. Ask Him to wash away all your sins and know that He is the Son of God. Amen! (Rom. 3:22-26)

I pray that you prayed that prayer, and I welcome you to our Father's kingdom! The angels are rejoicing over you, welcoming you in His presence! I pray that His healing is anointing and flowing wherever you may be. I pray that Jesus will touch you right now, wherever you are, and heal you from the top of your head to the soles of your feet. Let the anointing pour over you until your cup runneth over, just as it says in His word.

> *Surely he hath borne our griefs, and carried our sorrows: yet we did esteem Him stricken, smitten of God, and afflicted. But he was wounded for our transgressions; he was bruised for our iniquities: the chastisement of our peace was upon him; and with his stripes we are healed.* (Isa. 53:4-5) KJV

These following are scriptures that Jesus has blessed me with, and I would like to bless them to each of you and pray that the word of God will be poured into your spirit:

> *Trust in the Lord with all thine heart; and lean not unto thine own understanding. In all your ways acknowledge him, and he shall direct thy paths. Be not wise in thine own eyes: fear the Lord, and depart from evil. It shall be health to thy navel, and marrow to thy bones.* (Prov. 3:5) KJV

> *Length of days is in her right hand; and in her left hand riches and honour. Her ways are ways of pleasantness, and all her paths are peace. She is tree of life to them that lay hold upon her: and happy is everyone that retaineth her.* (Prov. 3:16-18) KJV

So shall they be life unto thy soul, and grace to thy neck then shalt thou walk in thy way safely, and thy foot shall not stumble. When thou liest down, thou shalt be afraid: yea, thou shalt lie down, and thy sleep shall be sweet. Be not afraid of sudden fear, neither of the desolation of the wicked, when it cometh. For the Lord shall be thy confidence, and shall keep thy foot from being taken. (Prov. 3:22-26) KJV

He taught me also, and said unto me, Let thine heart retain my words: keep my commandments and live. Get wisdom, get understanding: forget it not; neither decline from the words of my mouth. (Prov. 4:4-5) KJV

I have taught thee in the way of wisdom; I have led thee in right paths. When thou goest, thy steps shall not be straitened; and when thou runnest, thou shalt not stumble. Take fast hold of instructions; let her not go: keep her; for she is thy life. (Prov. 4:11-13) KJV

But he knoweth the way that I take: when he hath tried me, I shall come forth as gold. My foot hath held his steps, his way have I kept, and not declined. Neither have I gone back from the commandment of his lips; I have esteemed the words of his mouth more than my necessary food. But he is in one mind, and who can turn him? And what his soul desireth, even that he doeth. For he performeth the thing that is appointed for me: and many such things are with him. (Jobs 23:10-14) KJV

And not only so, but we glory in tribulations also: knowing that tribulation worketh patience; and patience, experience; and experience, hope: and hope maketh not ashamed; because the love of God is shed abroad in our hearts by the Holy Ghost which is given unto us. (Rom. 5:3-5) KJV

For though I be absent in the flesh, yet am I with you in the spirit, joying and beholding your order, and the steadfastness of your faith in Christ. (Col. 2:5) KJV

And after eight days again his disciples were within, and Thomas with them: then came Jesus, the doors being shut, and stood in the midst, and said, Peace be unto you. Then saith he to Thomas, reach hither thy finger, and behold my hands; and reach hither thy hand, and thrust it into my side: and be not faithless, but believe. (John 20:26-27) KJV

Jesus saith unto him, Thomas, because thou hast seen me, thou hast believed: blessed are they that have not seen, and yet have believed. (John 20:29) KJV

Yea doubtless, and I count all things but loss for the excellency of the knowledge of Christ Jesus my Lord: for whom I have suffered the loss of all things, and do count them but dung, that I may win Christ, and be found in him, not having mine own righteousness, which is of the law, but that which is through the faith of Christ, the righteousness which is of God by faith (Phil. 3:8-9) KJV

Rejoice in the Lord always: and again I say, Rejoice. Let your moderation be known unto all men. The Lord is at hand. Be careful for nothing; but in everything by prayer and supplication with thanksgiving let your requests be made known unto God. And the peace of God, which passeth all understanding, shall keep your hearts and minds through Christ Jesus. (Phil. 4:4-7) KJV

I can do all things through Christ which stregtheneth me. (Phil. 4:13) KJV

For the hope which is laid up for you in heaven, whereof ye heard before in the word of the truth of the gospel; which is come unto you, as it is in all the world; and bringeth forth fruit, as it doth also in you, since the day ye heard of it, and knew the grace of God in truth. (Col. 1:5-6) KJV

And he is before all things, and by him all things consist. (Col. 1:17) KJV

Put on therefore, as the elect of God, holy and beloved, bowels of mercies, kindness, humbleness of mind, meekness, longsuffering. Forbearing one another, and forgiving one another, if any man have a quarrel against any: even as Christ forgave you, so also do ye. And above all these things put on charity, which is the bond of perfectness. And let the peace of God rule in your hearts, to the which also ye are called in one body; and be ye thankful. Let the word of Christ dwell in you richly in all wisdom; teaching and admonishing one another in psalms and hymns and spiritual songs, singing with grace in your hearts to the Lord. And whatsoever ye do in word or deed, do all in the name of the Lord Jesus, giving thanks to God and the Father by him. (Col. 3:12-17) KJV

Wives, submit yourselves unto your own husbands, as it is fit in the Lord. Husbands, love your wives, and be not bitter against them. Children, obey your parents in all things: for this is well pleasing unto the Lord. Fathers, provoke not your children to anger, lest they be discouraged. Servants, obey in all things your master according to the flesh; not with eye service, as men pleasers; but in singleness of heart, fearing God. (Col. 3:18-22) KJV

Continue in prayer, and watch in the same with thanksgiving; withal praying also for us, that God would open unto us a door of utterance, to speak the mystery of Christ, for which I am also in bonds; That I may make it manifest, as I ought to speak. Walk in wisdom toward them that are without, redeeming the time. Let your speech be always with grace, seasoned with salt, that ye may know how ye ought to answer every man. (Col. 4:2-6) KJV

Buried with him in baptism, wherein also ye are risen with him through the faith of the operation of God, who hath raised him from the dead. And you, being dead in your sins and the uncircumcision of your flesh, hath he quickened tougher with him, having forgiven you all trespasses; blotting out the handwriting of ordinances that was against us, which was contrary to us, and took it out of the way, nailing it to his cross; and having spoiled principalities and powers, he made a shew of them openly, triumphing over them in it. Let no man therefore judge you in meat, or in drink, or in respect of an holy day, or of the new moon, or of the Sabbath days. (Col. 2:12-16) KJV

Wherefore comfort yourselves together, and edify one another, even as also ye do. (1 Thess. 5:11) KJV

Now our Lord Jesus Christ himself, and God, even our Father, which hath loved us, and hath given us everlasting consolation and good hope through grace, Comfort your hearts, and establish you in every good word and work. (2 Thess. 2:16-17) KJV

For I am with you the Lord that bringeth you up out of the land of Egypt, to be your God: ye shall therefore be holy, for I am Holy. (Lev. 11:45) KJV

My soul cleaveth unto the dust: quicken thou me according to thy word. I have declared my ways, and thou heardest me: teach me thy statutes. Make me to understand the way of thy precepts: so shall I talk of thy wondrous works. My soul melteth for heaviness: strengthen thou me according unto thy word. Remove from me the way of lying: and grant me thy law graciously. I have chosen the way of truth: thy judgments have I laid before me. I have stuck unto thy testimonies: O Lord, put me not to shame. I will run the way of thy commandments, when thou shalt enlarge my heart. (Ps. 119:25-32) KJV

Let thy tender mercies come unto me, that I may live: for thy law is my delight. (Ps. 119:77) KJV

The fear of the Lord is the beginning of wisdom: and the knowledge of the holy is understanding. For by me thy days shall be multiplied, and the years of thy life shall be increased. If thou be wise, thou shalt be wise for thyself: but if thou scornest, thou alone shalt bear it. (Prov. 9:10-12) KJV

For they shall be an ornament of grace unto thy head, and chains about thy neck. (Prov. 1:9) KJV

Trust in the Lord with all thine heart; and lean not unto thine own understanding. In all thy ways acknowledge him, and he shall direct thy paths be not wise in thine own eyes: fear the Lord, and depart from evil. It shall be health to thy navel, and marrow to thy bones. (Prov. 3:5-8) KJV

Length of days is in her right hand; and in her left hand riches and honour. Her ways are ways of pleasantness, and all her paths are peace. She is a tree of life to them that lay hold upon her: and happy is every one that retaineth her. The Lord by wisdom hath founded the earth; by understanding hath he established the heavens. (Prov. 3:16-18) KJV

When thou vowest a vow unto God, defer not to pay it; for he hath no pleasure in fools: pay that which thou hast vowed. Better is it that thou shouldest not vow, than that thou shouldest vow and not pay. Suffer not thy mouth to cause thy flesh to sin; neither say thou before the angel that was an error: wherefore should God be angry at thy voice, and destroy the work of thine hands? For in the multitude of dreams and many words there are also divers vanities: but fear thou God. (Eccles. 5:4-7) KJV

Whoso keepeth the commandment shall feel no evil thing: and a wise man's heart discerneth both time judgment. Because to every purpose there is time and judgment, therefore the misery of man is great upon him. For he knoweth not that which shall be: for who can tell him when it shall be? There is no man that hath power over the spirit to retain the spirit; neither hath he power in the day of death: and there is no discharge in that war; neither shall wickedness deliver those that are given to it. (Eccles. 8:5-8) KJV

Remember now thy Creator in the days of thy youth, while the evil days come not, nor the years draw nigh, when thou shalt say, I have no pleasure in them. (Eccles. 12:1) KJV

The thief cometh not, but for to steal, and to kill, and to destroy: I have come that they might have life, and that they might have it more abundantly. (John 10:10) KJV

Therefore hath the Lord recompensed me according to my righteousness, according to the cleanness of my hands in his eyesight. (Ps. 18:24) KJV

I create the fruit of the lips; Peace, peace to him that is far off, and him that is near, saith the Lord; and I will heal him. (Isa. 57:19) KJV

Then shalt thou call, and the Lord shall answer; thou shalt cry, and he shall say, here I am. If thou take away from the midst of thee the yoke, the putting forth of the finger, and speaking vanity. (Isa. 58:9) KJV

And the Lord shall guide thee continually, and satisfy thy soul in drought, and make fat thy bones: and thou shalt be like a watered garden, and like a spring of water, whose waters fail not. (Isa. 58:11) KJV

If thou turn away thy foot from the Sabbath, from doing thy pleasure on my holy day; and call the Sabbath a delight, the holy of the Lord, honorable; and shalt honor him, not doing thine own ways, nor finding thine own pleasure, nor speaking thine own words; then shalt thou delight thyself in the Lord; and I will cause thee to ride upon the high places of the earth, and feed thee with the heritage of Jacob thy father: for the mouth of the Lord hath spoken it. (Isa. 58:13-14) KJV

For your shame ye shall have double; and for confusion they shall rejoice in their portion: therefore in their land they shall possess the double: everlasting joy shall be unto them. (Isa. 61:7) KJV

And I will restore to you the years that the locust hath eaten, the cankerworm, and the caterpillar, and the palmerworm, my great army which I sent among you. (Joel 2:25) KJV

So the Lord blessed the latter end of Job more than his beginning: for he had fourteen thousand sheep, and six thousand camels, and a thousand sheep, and six thousand camels, and a thousand yoke of oxen, and a thousand she asses. (Job 42:12) KJV

And the Lord said, I have surely seen the affliction of my people in Egypt, and have heard their cry by reason of their taskmasters; for I know their sorrows; and I am come down to deliver them out of the hand of the Egyptians, and to bring them up out of that land unto a good land and a large, unto a land flowing with milk and honey; unto the place of the Canaanites, and Hittites, and Amorites, and Perizzites, and Hivites, and the Jebusites. (Exod. 3:7-8) KJV

And if a house be divided against itself, that house cannot stand. (Mark 3:25) KJV

Now get up. Stand on your feet. I have appeared to you to appoint you to serve me and be my witness. You will tell others that you have seen me today. You will also tell them that I will show myself to you again I will save you from your own people and from those who aren't Jews. I am sending you to them. To open their eyes. I want you to turn them from darkness to light. I want you to turn them from Satan's power to God. I want their sins to be forgiven. They will be forgiven when they believe in me. They will have their place among God's people. (Acts 26:16-18) NIRV

One night the Lord spoke to Paul in a vision and told him, "Do not be afraid; keep on speaking, do not be silent. For I am with you, and no one is going to attack and harm you, because I have many people in this city." (Acts 18:9-10) NIV

He said to them, "Go into all the world and preach the gospel to all creation. Whoever believes and is baptized will be saved, but whoever does not believe will be condemned. And these signs will accompany those who believe: in my name they will drive out demons; they will speak in new tongues; they will pick up snakes with their hands; and when they drink deadly poison, it will not hurt them at all; they will place their hands on sick people, and the will get well."" (Mark 16:15-18) NIV

David said about him: "I saw the Lord always before me. Because he is at my right hand, I will not be shaken. Therefore my heart is glad and my tongue rejoices; my body also will rest in hope, because you will not abandon me to the realm of the dead, you will not let your holy one see decay. You have made known to me the paths of life; you will fill me with joy in your presence."" (Act 2:25-28) NIV

Jesus replied, "All those who love me will do what I say. My Father will love them, and will come to them and live with them. Anyone who doesn't love me will not do what do what I say. And remember, my words are not my own. This message is from the Father who sent me. I am telling you these things now while I am still with you. But when the Father sends the Counselor as my representative and by the Counselor I mean the Holy Spirit he will teach you everything and will remind you of everything I myself have told you." "I am leaving you with a gift peace of mind and heart." And the peace I give isn't like the peace the world gives. So don't be troubled or afraid. (John 14:23-27) NIV

Death and life are in the power of the tongue: and they that love it shall eat the fruit thereof. (Prov. 18:21) KJV

Do not neglect your gift, which was given you through a prophetic message when the body of elders laid their hands on you. (1 Tim. 4:14) NIV

Heal the sick who are there and tell them, "The Kingdom of God is near you." (Luke 10:9) NIV

Be diligent in these matters; give yourself wholly to them, so that everyone may see your progress. (1 Tim. 4:15) NIV

My son, pay attention to what I say; turn your ear to my words. Do not let them out of your sight, keep them within your heart. (Prov. 4:20-21) NIV

Do not be wise in your own eyes fear the Lord and shun evil. This will bring health to your body and nourishment to your bones. (Prov. 3:7-8) NIV

This day I call heaven and earth as witnesses against you that I have set before you life, and death, blessings and curses. Now choose life, so that you and your children may live. And that you may love the Lord your God, listen to his voice, and hold fast to him. For the Lord is your life, and he will give you many years in land he swore to give to your fathers, Abraham, Isaac, and Jacob. (Deut. 30:19-20) NIV

God's voice thunders in marvelous way; he does great things beyond our understanding. (Job 37:5) NIV

The king rejoices in your strength,Lord. How great is his joy in the victories you give!. (Ps. 21:1) NIV

Guard my life and rescue me; do not let me not be put to shame, for I take refuge in you. (Ps. 25:20) NIV

Long life is in her right hand; in her left hand are riches and honor.,. Her ways are pleasant ways, and all her paths are peace. She is a tree of life to those who take hold of her; those who hold her fast will be blessed. (Prov. 3:16-18) NIV

The fear of the Lord is the beginning of wisdom, and knowledge of the holy one is understanding. For through me your days will be many, and years will be added to your life. (Prov. 9:10-11) NIV

Be ever hearing, but never understanding; be ever seeing but never perceiving. Make the heart of this people calloused; make their ears dull and close their eyes. Otherwise they might see with their eyes, hear with their hearts and turn and be healed. (Isa. 6:9-10) NIV

The Lord will save me, and we will sing with stringed instruments all the days of our lives in the temple of the Lord. (Isa. 38:20) NIV

I have seen their ways, but I will heal them; I will guide them and restore comfort to Isreal's mourners,. creating praise on the lips. Peace, peace, to those far and near says the Lord and I will heal them. (Isa. 57:18-19) NIV

71

The Lord your God is with you, the Mighty Warrior who saves. He will take great delight in you;, in his love he will no longer rebuke you. But will rejoice over you with singing. (Zeph. 3:17) NIV

I ask you, therefore, not to be discouraged because of my sufferings for you, which are your glory. (Eph. 3:13) NIV

Then the Lord answered and said to me write down the vision I give you so those on the path of life can read and understand it. The vision may be for the future, but eventually you will see the completion of the vision. (Hab. 2:2-3) NIV

Delight yourself in the Lord and he will give you the desires of your heart. Commit your way to the Lord; trust in him and he will do this. He will make your righteousness shine like the dawn, the justice of your cause like the noon day sun. Be still before the Lord and wait patiently for him. (Ps. 37:4-7) NIV

Trust in the Lord with all your heart and lean not on your on understanding. In all your ways acknowledge him and he will make your paths straight. (Prov. 3:5-6) NIV

A person's steps are directed by the Lord. How then can anyone understand their own way? (Prov. 20:24) NIV

I took you from the ends of the earth, from its farthest corners I called you. I said, "you are my servant"; I have chosen you and have not rejected you. So do not fear, for I am with you; do not be dismayed, for I am your God. I will strengthen you and help you; I will uphold you with my righteous right hands. (Isa. 41:9-10) NIV

God is not a man, that he should lie; nor a son of man, that he should repent: hath He said, and shall he not do it? Or hath he spoken, and shall he not make it good? (Num. 23:19) KJV

One of them, when he saw he was healed, came back, praising God in a loud voice. He threw himself at Jesus' feet and thanked him and he was a Samaritan. Jesus asked, "Were not all ten cleansed? Where are the other nine? Has no one returned to give praise to God except this foreigner? Then he said to him, "Rise and go; your faith has made you well.". (Luke 17:15-19) NIV

He himself bore our sins in his body on the tree, so that we might die to sins and live for righteousness; by his wounds you have been healed. 1 Pet. 2:24NIV

Heal me, O Lord, and I will be healed; save me and I will be saved, for you are the one I praise.

They keep saying to me "Where is the word of the Lord?" Let it now be fulfilled. (Jer. 17:14-15) NIV

But blessed is the man who trusts in the Lord, whose confidence is in him. He will be like a tree planted by the water that sends out its roots by the stream it does not fear when heat comes; its leaves are always green. It has no worries in a year of drought and never fails to bear fruit. (Jer. 17:7-8) NIV

All the nations may walk in the name of their gods; we will walk in the name of the LORD our God for ever and ever. (Mic. 4:5) NIV

In a large house there are articles not only of gold and silver, but also of wood and clay; some are for noble purposes and some for ignoble. If a man cleansehimself from the latter, he will be an instrument for noble purposes to do any good work. Flee the evil desire of youth, and pursue righteousness, faith, love, and peace along with those who call on the lord out of a pure heart. (2 Tim. 2:20-22) NIV

Turn to me and be saved all you ends of the earth; for I am God, and there is no other. (Isa. 45:22) NIV

Even to your old age and gray hairs I am he, I am he who will sustain you I have made you and I will carry you I will sustain you and I will rescue you. (Isa. 46:4) NIV

You are my lamp. O Lord the lord turns my darkness into light. (2 Sam. 22:29) NIV

It is God who arms me with strength and makes my way perfect. (2 Sam. 22:33) NIV

The fear of the LORD is the beginning of wisdom, and knowledge of the Holy One is understanding.

For through me your days will be many, and years will be added to your life. (Prov. 9:10-11) NIV

When the storm has swept by, the wicked are gone, but the righteous stand firm forever. (Prov. 10:25) NIV

I guide you in the way of wisdom and lead you along straight paths. When you walk, your steps will not be hampered; when you run you will not stumble. Hold on to instruction, do not let it go; guard it well, for it is your life. (Prov. 4:11-13) NIV

For God's gifts and his call are irrevocable. (Rom. 11:29) NIV

Blessed are all who fear the Lord who walk in his ways, you will eat the fruits of your labor blessings and prosperity will be yours. Your wife will be like a fruitful vine within your house your sons will be like olive shoots around your table. Thus is the man blessed who fears the Lord. May you see the prosperity of Jerusalem, and may you live to see your children's children. (Ps. 128:1-6) NKJV

But what could I say? For he himself had sent this sickness. Now I will walk humbly throughout my years because of this anguish I have felt. Lord, your discipline is good, for it leads to life and health. You have restored my health and have let me live! Yes, it was good for me to suffer this anguish, for you have rescued me from death and have forgiven all my sins. For the dead cannot praise you; they cannot raise their voices in praise. Those who go down to destruction can no longer hope in your faithfulness. Only the living can praise you as I do today. Each generation an make known your faithfulness to the next. Think of it the Lord has healed me! I will sing praises with instruments every day of my life in the temple of the Lord. (Isa. 38:15-20) NIV

About the Author

Regina Reyna is a servant of the Lord, loves Jesus, and wants to share her testimony with many souls. Regina loves serving in the nursery and teaching her children about the word of God. She has a wonderful husband, Rene Reyna, who has been with her through everything. He is faithful and a true man of God. She has four beautiful children: David, who is now eight; Emmanuel and Eliana, who are both two; and the baby in the family, Joshua, is one. She feels blessed to have such a wonderful family.

About the Book

My journey with Jesus began in Germany. I was diagnosed with breast cancer and had to go through the trial of chemotherapy and radiation. Jesus told me that this sickness was not to harm me but to purify me and that I would awe and astonish the doctors. This testimony is about how Jesus healed me and set me free. This story is all about Jesus, not about me. Jesus is no respecter person. If He did it for me, He can and will do it for you. So come along and hear about the awesome Jesus I serve. I pray that you will embrace Him in your heart and let Him touch you like never before. Come meet my King!